What Is the Statue of Liberty?

by Joan Holub

illustrated by John Hinderliter

Penguin Workshop

To big ideas—JH

Always stay curious. Thanks, Dad—JH

PENGUIN WORKSHOP
An Imprint of Penguin Random House LLC, New York

Text copyright © 2014 by Joan Holub.
Illustrations copyright © 2014 by Penguin Random House LLC. All rights reserved.
Published by Penguin Workshop, an imprint of Penguin Random House LLC, New York.
PENGUIN and PENGUIN WORKSHOP are trademarks of Penguin Books Ltd.
WHO HQ & Design is a registered trademark of Penguin Random House LLC.
Printed in the USA.

Visit us online at www.penguinrandomhouse.com.

Library of Congress Control Number: 2014939726

ISBN 9780448479170   20 19

Contents

What Is the Statue of Liberty?

In July 1976, the United States had a holiday. It was the two-hundredth anniversary of the signing of the Declaration of Independence. All over the country, towns and cities celebrated. In New York City, there were fireworks, parades, and patriotic speeches. Right in the middle of it all stood that towering symbol of American freedom—the Statue of Liberty!

The statue's real name is *Liberty Enlightening the World*, but it's often called Lady Liberty or the Statue of Liberty. The statue is huge—151 feet and 1 inch tall. That's about as tall as a tower of thirty-five eleven-year-old kids stacked head-to-toe.

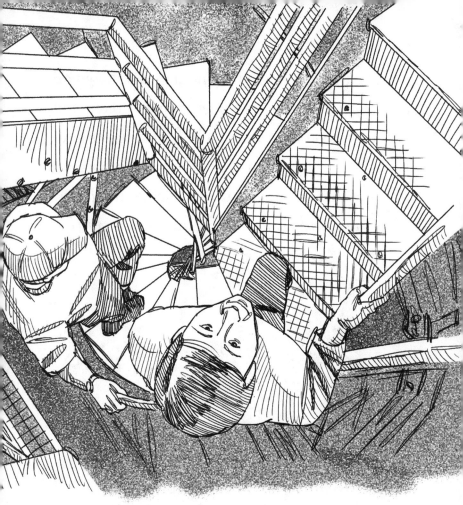

It's made of copper and is mostly hollow, with a metal skeleton-like support structure inside and stairs so visitors can walk up into its crown. Today about four million people visit the Statue of Liberty and Ellis Island every year.

Like the American flag, the statue is shown on army posters and on postage stamps. A picture of the torch is on the ten dollar bill. Advertisers have used it to sell everything from soap to hamburgers. It has even had roles in movies such as the *Planet of the Apes, Independence Day,* and *Superman II.*

Since 1886, the statue has offered a message of hope to immigrants coming to America. From the late 1800s into the 1900s, millions came from other countries. Most were very poor and most came from Europe. They crossed the Atlantic Ocean on steamships. As the majority of those ships sailed into New York Harbor, one of the first landmarks they saw was the Statue of Liberty. They would cheer and sometimes cry with joy. At last they had reached America, land of liberty, where they hoped to start a new and better life.

During World Wars I and II, American soldiers from all over the US were sent to New York City. There, they boarded ships bound for European battlefields. As they departed, they sailed past the statue. It inspired patriotic feelings in so many of them. And when soldiers returned after the wars, the statue was there to welcome them home.

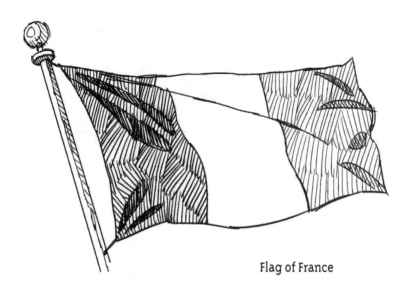

Flag of France

Surprisingly, the Statue of Liberty was not the United States' idea. It was a gift from the people of France. A French professor first proposed the idea, a French sculptor designed the statue, and a French engineer designed its inner framework. Americans were not even sure they wanted the statue at first. Some were suspicious about the reasons behind the gift. They almost said no to France!

CHAPTER 1
The Big Idea

It all started in 1865 at a dinner party outside Paris, France. At least, that's the legend that was printed in a fundraising brochure for the Statue of Liberty twenty years later. The party was held in the home of a law professor named Edouard de Laboulaye. He was an expert on American history.

He'd written books about the American way of government. He thought all countries should be like the United States—free to elect their own government leaders.

The Civil War had just ended in America. Laboulaye had admired President Abraham Lincoln for bringing slavery to an end and uniting all the states again after the war. This was a sign that the democratic form of government was strong. In the end, it had worked well even during troubled times.

Just as the thirteen American colonies had once risen up against the king of England, so too had the French people rebelled against their king. The French Revolution had begun in 1789, only thirteen years after Americans proclaimed their independence. Unfortunately, unlike the American Revolution, the French Revolution ended in disaster. Instead of becoming a free country, France was ruled by a series of emperors.

Their word was law. The French people couldn't say anything against the government without getting in big trouble.

Laboulaye wanted to make a statement in support of political freedom, but he needed to do it in a way that wouldn't put him in danger. He couldn't help but dream: What if France gave America an amazing monument that celebrated liberty?

One of Laboulaye's dinner guests that night was a sculptor. His name was Frédéric-Auguste

Bartholdi. He liked to work big. He'd gone to see the pyramids and the Sphinx in Egypt. These gigantic ancient monuments really had impressed him. He wasn't quite as interested in American politics as Laboulaye, but he loved his statue idea and volunteered to sculpt it.

The French Revolution

King Louis XVI of France helped American colonists win independence from England in 1783. The American war cost France a lot of money. His wife, Queen Marie Antoinette, liked to buy fancy clothes and jewels, and threw big parties. While the king and queen spent the country's riches as they pleased, poor French people were starving. On July 14, 1789, the French Revolution began when Paris citizens broke into Bastille prison and stole weapons to fight the king and his government. The French revolutionaries got together and wrote their own Declaration of Independence, which they called the Declaration of the Rights of Man. Soon the battles became bloody and violent. In 1793, the king and queen were beheaded by guillotine. Rich, powerful people were thought to be the enemies of everyday French people. Over 17,000

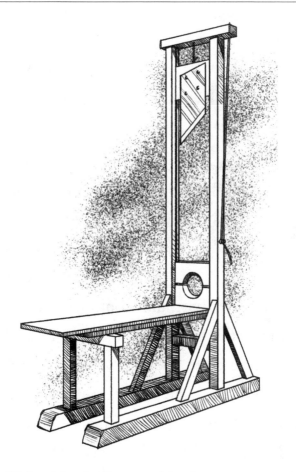

politicians, landowners, and business owners were put on trial and executed. Many were beheaded. In 1799, a general in the French army named Napoleon Bonaparte rose to power and the revolution ended.

Of course, Bartholdi knew just as well as Laboulaye that such a statue could land them in jail. They'd be arrested by Emperor Napoleon III's secret police. Their idea was put on hold, but not forgotten.

Meanwhile, Bartholdi took a second trip to Egypt in 1869. He hoped to design a lighthouse at the entrance to the newly built Suez Canal, which connected the Mediterranean Sea to the Red Sea. It would be no ordinary lighthouse: It would be in the shape of a woman. He wanted to name it *Egypt Bringing the Light to Asia.* Besides actually lighting the way for ships, his statue would symbolize Egypt leading the way to new ideas.

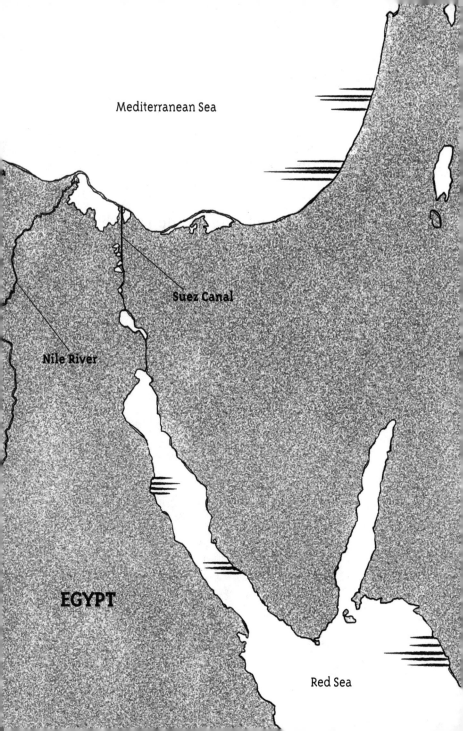

Bartholdi quickly made sketches and models of the statue. Egypt's ruler liked the project. However, Egypt didn't have the money to build it. Many historians think Bartholdi based the Statue of Liberty on his ideas for the Suez Canal lighthouse. He never would say why he had done both designs as women in ancient-style clothes, or why both wear crowns and hold a torch high in one hand.

By 1870, Napoleon III was no longer in power. Laboulaye hoped that now a democracy would take root in France. Presenting a statue in honor of liberty to America might inspire the French to work toward a liberal, elected government of their own. He knew that building a gigantic statue would cost a lot of money. Would his fellow citizens think it was worth it?

What about Americans? What would they think of the idea? Would they agree to accept the statue? Would they offer a suitable piece of land where the statue could be displayed? Bartholdi decided to go find out.

Laboulaye and Bartholdi

Laboulaye was born on January 18, 1811, in Paris, France. Not only was he an expert on US history, but he also taught the very first class about the US Constitution at a French college. He believed that every person had the right to be free, and would likely be happy that people in France are now free to elect their political leaders.

Bartholdi was born into a prosperous family on August 2, 1834, in Colmar, France. His father died when he was two years old and his family moved to Paris. His mother encouraged his studies in art.

Although Laboulaye came up with the idea for the Statue of Liberty, it was Bartholdi who became world famous as its creator. His second most famous sculpture is the Lion of Belfort, a seventy-two-foot-long sandstone lion. It's in the town of Belfort, France, about forty-five miles from where Bartholdi was born.

CHAPTER 2
Bedloe's Island

Bartholdi set out for the United States in June of 1871. He was to meet with important people in America that Laboulaye knew—rich men and politicians. They were the kind of people who could make big things happen—like a big statue. As Bartholdi's ship sailed into New York Harbor, he spotted Bedloe's Island. A star-shaped fort stood on the island.

NEW JERSEY

Hudson River

Manhattan

East River

Ellis Island

Bedloe's Island

Governor's Island

Brooklyn

New York Harbor

This was the perfect spot for his dream statue. Standing in the harbor of the biggest city in the US, it would be seen by millions of people. This location would be so much better than a smaller harbor, a park, or a city plaza. Bartholdi grew more and more excited. He hadn't even set foot on American soil yet, and he'd already found the right home for his statue!

President
Ulysses S. Grant

Frédéric-Auguste
Bartholdi

For the next few months, Bartholdi visited Laboulaye's friends in cities across the US. People welcomed him everywhere he went. He met the poet Henry Wadsworth Longfellow and Brigham Young, the leader of the Mormon Church. When he met President Ulysses S. Grant, Bartholdi asked if his statue could be built on Bedloe's Island, but nothing was decided for sure. Bartholdi told everyone about the statue. He was charming and a good salesman. Everyone liked him, but that didn't mean they liked his idea. It sounded farfetched—like a dream that would never come true. Still, his visit did get Americans talking about his statue.

When Bartholdi returned to France, he was more enthusiastic than ever. He couldn't stop thinking about Bedloe's Island. Before his trip, he'd made some sketches of how his statue might look. He'd even made small model statues in terracotta, a kind of clay used in pottery. These looked very much like his Suez lighthouse models.

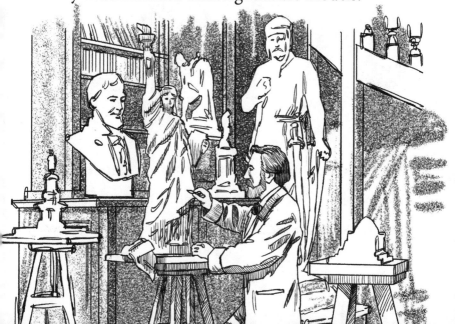

In fact, his plan was to make his new liberty statue a lighthouse, too. Perhaps he hoped that such a useful statue might appeal to Americans. At first, he wasn't sure whether to light the crown or the torch. But now that he'd found the perfect place for his statue, it was time to finalize his design.

He studied how other artists had painted figures and scenes representing the idea of liberty. He looked at old coins stamped with a picture of the Roman goddess Libertas. He read about a famous

ancient statue called the Colossus of Rhodes. He read books about the ancient monuments of Egypt that he so admired. Then he spent the next few months making more clay models. If he could show people exactly what the statue was going to look like, maybe they'd become as excited about the project as he was.

The Colossus of Rhodes

In ancient times, tourists spread the word about amazing sights they'd visited. The most famous became known as the Seven Wonders of the Ancient World. A structure on the Greek island of Rhodes was one of them. At about one hundred feet tall, it was a colossus—a very tall statue. It was designed in the shape of the Greek sun god, Helios. It was made of iron and bronze, and its legs were filled with stones for support. It probably held a torch or lamp in one hand and a spear in its other hand and stood at the entrance to a harbor. Some old drawings show the god statue standing with legs spread wide, so that ships could sail between them. An earthquake destroyed the Colossus in 226 BC, so today no one is sure exactly what it looked like.

CHAPTER 3
Designing the Statue

Stola

Palla

Bartholdi's favorite final design showed Liberty as a woman dressed like a Roman goddess, in a long gown with sleeves called a *stola*. Over that, she wore a *palla*, which is a cape that's held on by a clasp at the left shoulder. There were sandals on her feet.

The statue's right arm is raised high and holds a torch. The crown has seven long pointed rays to represent the seven continents and the seven seas. The hairstyle was done in 1800s fashion. As Bartholdi made more models, the statue's face began to look more determined and stern. Although it looked a lot like his mother, Bartholdi never would say for sure that it was her face.

Charlotte Bartholdi

In some of Bartholdi's models, the Statue of Liberty held a broken chain and shackle in her left hand. It represented freedom. However, he worried that everyone's eyes would be drawn to the chain more than anything else, so he placed the broken shackle and chain at the statue's feet.

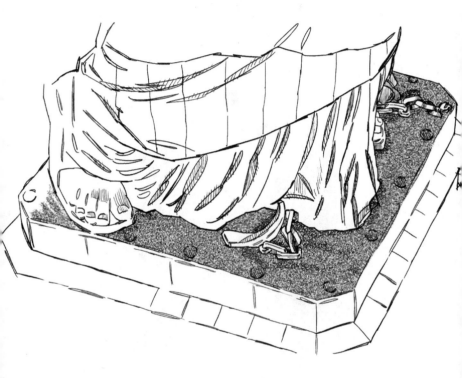

The heel of Liberty's right foot is raised as if the statue is stepping out of the broken chains toward freedom. In the statue's left hand, Bartholdi put a tablet with a date carved in Roman numerals:

July 4, 1776, America's
Independence Day.

As Bartholdi made
more models, they got
bigger and bigger. In his
opinion, the best was
the one he made in early
1875. Laboulaye liked it,
too. It was about four-and-a-half feet tall and was
made of plaster. This is the model on which the
real statue was based. Enlarging his model to stand
over 151 feet tall would not be easy. Thousands
of very careful measurements and exact math
calculations would have to be done. He would
need the help of carpenters, metalworkers, and
other craftsmen. These workers would have to be
paid.

To raise money, Laboulaye formed a
committee called the French-American Union.
They approved Bartholdi's statue design.

On November 6, 1875, a fancy dinner party was held for two hundred rich guests near the famous Louvre Museum in Paris. Bartholdi's plaster statue model was unveiled. The guests were so excited to see it that they donated about $25,000. The trouble was that building the statue would cost ten times that much.

Major publicity was needed to get people to donate more money. America's one-hundredth birthday was coming up in 1876. To celebrate it, there was going to be a World's Fair—the first one ever held in the US. The fair would be in Philadelphia, where the Declaration of Independence had been signed.

There wasn't enough time or money to build the whole Statue of Liberty to exhibit at the fair. But Bartholdi and Laboulaye came up with a brilliant plan. They would finish one part of the statue, and they would exhibit it in Philadelphia.

They decided on the hand and its torch. But could they even get that much ready in time?

CHAPTER 4
The Hand with the Torch

Bartholdi decided to work with Gaget, Gauthier & Cie, a Paris company that had a metal workshop. Most statues were made of bronze, marble, or stone. On the advice of his former teacher, Eugène Viollet-le-Duc, Bartholdi decided to use copper. Copper was cheaper and lighter in weight. It was easy to hammer and wouldn't crack when it was bent. He would build his statue as a copper shell and would figure out a support structure to put inside it later on.

To start, workers doubled the size of Bartholdi's favorite model to make a plaster copy of it that stood about nine-and-a-half feet tall. After that, they made an even bigger model at about thirty-eight feet tall. Multiplying it by four again, they

6 feet

9.5 feet

38 feet

151 feet

planned to enlarge the statue to its final size of over 151 feet tall. There was no way to fit a statue that tall inside the workshop.

Instead, they decided to cut the thirty-eight-foot plaster model into eight horizontal sections that were like the layers of a cake. Then they measured each layer separately using rulers, compasses, and strings that hung down from overhead to various points on its surface. Using these measurements, they enlarged each layer to full size. Later, they would put everything together.

The first order of business was making the full-size hand and torch. Carpenters built many wooden molds around the plaster model of the hand-and-torch part. The molds were made to fit snugly against it. When they were shaped just right, the molds were removed.

Next, large flat sheets of copper were heated in ovens and with simple blowtorches to soften them. The copper was only about one-tenth of an inch thick—the thickness of two stacked pennies. Workers pressed a copper sheet inside each wood mold. *Whack!* They carefully hammered the copper sheet so it bent and curved to match the mold's shape. This process is called repoussé, a French word that means "push back." It took twenty-one sheets of copper to make the hand and torch. It was going

to take over three hundred copper sheets for the entire Statue of Liberty!

The start of the Philadelphia fair was fast approaching. The workshop was loud with banging hammers as twenty men worked seven days a week for months. Still, the hand-and-torch part was not ready in time. This really disappointed Bartholdi. In May of 1876, he reluctantly sailed off to the United States without a piece of his statue. He hoped it would arrive soon after the opening ceremonies.

Two hundred temporary buildings had been

created just for the Philadelphia fair, including a glass-walled exhibition hall. It covered over twenty-one acres, making it the biggest building in the world at the time. Exhibits from the United States were in the middle of the hall, with other countries' exhibits around them. There were meteorites, Native American tools and art, and exotic animals including a stuffed walrus and polar bear. A new invention called the telephone

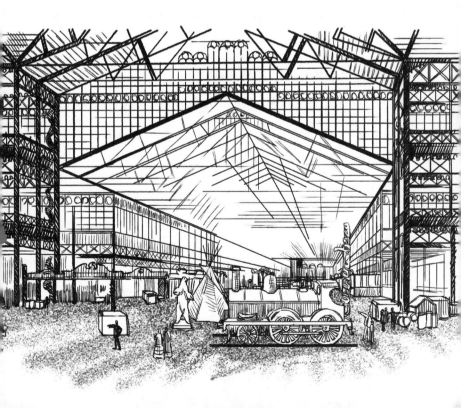

was on display. People had never seen such fantastic sights! About ten million visitors came to the fair. That was equal to about one-fifth of the entire US population in the 1870s.

As for the hand and torch, they didn't arrive until August. Visitors paid fifty cents to climb a ladder through the inside of the forearm. Twelve to fifteen people at a time could stand outside on the balcony that ringed the torch. The hand and torch stood as tall as a three-story building. The hand's fingernail measured ten inches by thirteen inches. There was a painting of what the entire statue would look like on the base below the torch.

Visitors must have been awestruck, imagining how huge the finished statue would be. Bartholdi's exhibit was a sensation!

CHAPTER 5
The Head

When the Philadephia fair ended on November 10, 1876, the hand and torch went to New York City. The part stood in Madison Square Park for over five years while the rest of the statue was being built in Paris.

The US Congress voted in 1877 to accept France's statue as a gift. Bedloe's Island was chosen as the site. The US also agreed to build a strong base called a pedestal for Liberty to stand on. This must have been a huge relief to Bartholdi. His statue would officially have a home in the US when it was finished.

For the Paris Universal Exposition in 1878, Bartholdi's crew finished the statue's head. It was loaded onto a big wagon filled with hay and small branches to cushion it. Thirteen strong horses pulled the wagon across Paris to the fairground.

The statue's head was showcased in the garden of a palace that had been built just for the fair. Visitors paid a donation to the statue fund to climb to the top of the head. Thirty to forty people could stand inside it and gaze out through the row of twenty-five windows in its crown. Its nose was four-and-a-half feet long. Each eye was two-and-a-half feet wide. It must have been a thrilling sight to experience!

By 1879, the statue's fundraising committee had about half the money they needed. Bartholdi worked hard to raise even more. He told French businesses that his statue would surely become a great American symbol. He convinced them to pay money to use the statue's image on their products.

There were lotteries where people could buy chances to win money and prizes. There were charity events like operas, with proceeds going into the fund. Small souvenir copies of the statue were sold, some autographed by Bartholdi himself. By July 1880, the fundraising committee had raised 400,000 francs in all. That was about $250,000 back then. It was enough!

Over at the Paris shop, about forty men continued working on the statue's eight layers. Each layer was about twelve feet tall and thirty feet wide. The amount of copper used was enough to make thirty million pennies!

The World's Tallest Statues

The 420-foot-tall Spring Temple Buddha in Henan, China, is the tallest statue in the world.

Three other statues may someday rise even taller. The Statue of Unity in Gujarat, India, is planned to be 597 feet tall. The 563-foot Crazy Horse Memorial is being carved from rock in the Black Hills of South Dakota in the US. The Garuda Wisnu Kencana statue in Bali, Indonesia, will be 479 feet tall.

CHAPTER 6
The Statue's Guts

Things were going great, but there still was one problem. Until that point, Bartholdi had been using temporary wood frames inside each of the statue sections for support. He knew that kind of frame wouldn't be strong enough for the enormous entire statue when it was finished.

It was time to hire an engineer to come up with a support structure that would fit inside the statue and hold it up. Bartholdi decided on Eugène Viollet-le-Duc. Viollet-le-Duc thought that weighing the statue down was the best plan. He suggested filling the statue from its hips to its feet with big, heavy boxes of sand. This idea probably would not have worked. In any case, Viollet-le-Duc died before he could try it.

Next, Bartholdi turned to Gustave Eiffel for help. Later, Eiffel would build the world-famous Eiffel Tower in Paris, but he was already famous for building railroad bridges out of iron beams. Big bridges had always been built of stone. Eiffel had discovered that iron-beam bridges could support more weight than stone. At the time, this was a brand-new idea. He decided that Bartholdi's copper shell statue would remain hollow except for a strong iron skeleton hidden inside it. It would work in somewhat the same way as a human skeleton.

Eiffel Tower

Gustave Eiffel built his 985-foot-tall Eiffel Tower for the Paris World Fair in 1889 on the one-hundredth anniversary of the French Revolution. The tower had an open framework of iron beams like Eiffel's bridges. There were elevators to take visitors to different levels. Altogether, it used 7,300 tons of iron, sixty tons of paint, and 2.5 million rivets—eight times the number in the Statue of Liberty.

At first, people made fun of it. They'd never seen anything like it. Some people thought it looked like an overgrown street lamp or strange-looking gym equipment. During the fair, ten thousand lights decorated the tower. At night it looked beautiful and romantic. The tower was considered a masterpiece! Two million visitors came to see it during the World's Fair, including Buffalo Bill and Thomas Edison. Today, about seven million people visit the Eiffel Tower

every year. It was almost torn down in 1909, but was turned into a radio tower instead. It was taller than any building in the world until New York's 1,250-foot Empire State Building was finished in 1931.

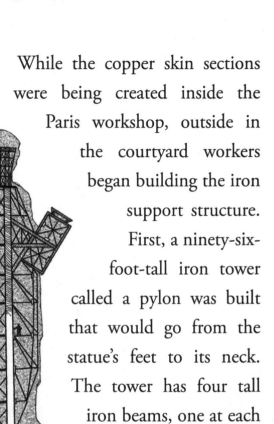

While the copper skin sections were being created inside the Paris workshop, outside in the courtyard workers began building the iron support structure.

First, a ninety-six-foot-tall iron tower called a pylon was built that would go from the statue's feet to its neck. The tower has four tall iron beams, one at each corner. Cross braces that looked like big X's connect the beams.

On top of this, a smaller iron frame was built for the head. Another long iron support frame for the arm holding the torch angles from where the shoulder would be. A double spiral staircase was built in the center of the statue skeleton, with one set of steps for going up and another for going down. The stairs go all the way into the head, and a ladder leads up into the torch.

Thin iron bars are bolted on one side all along the pylon, so that they poke out toward the copper skin. The far ends of each of these bars are bolted to horizontal rib bars braced along the inside of the statue's copper-sheet skin. This kind of connection system means that no sheet of copper skin weighs down on the one below it. Instead, the thin iron bars transfer the weight of each copper sheet back to the strong pylon tower. The first skyscrapers would be built using this method just a few years later.

When the whole iron support frame was ready, workers started adding the shaped copper sheets. They began at the feet and worked their way up, fitting the copper sheets together like a patchwork quilt to form the statue's skin. Temporary screws were used to hold them in place for now. Rivets, which were like big nails, would be used later when the statue went to its final location in New York. By July 1882, Bartholdi's statue was covered with copper up to its waist.

Eight months earlier, an architect named Richard Morris Hunt had been chosen to design an enormous pedestal in New York. It would be the base on which the statue would stand.

Hunt was known for building mansions for rich families like the Vanderbilts. Like Bartholdi, he thought big. His first pedestal idea was 114 feet tall. It would be made of solid granite and would have cost about $250,000. The American fundraising committee only had donations of a third that much. His design was just too expensive, and it was rejected.

Vanderbilt
Mansion

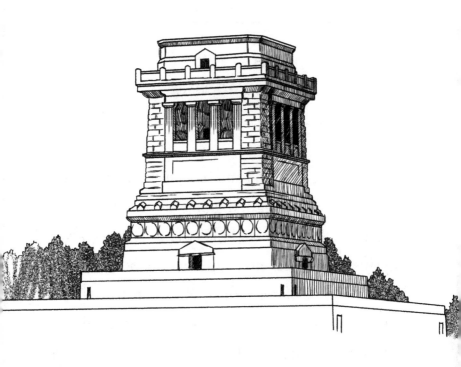

Hunt redesigned his pedestal. Eventually, it was shortened to eighty-nine feet. It would be built of concrete and covered with a layer of granite. That would bring the cost down.

CHAPTER 7
The Pedestal

Once the fundraising committee approved Hunt's pedestal design, digging began on Bedloe's Island in 1883. A huge hole twenty feet deep was dug inside the eleven-point, star-shaped walls of Fort Wood. Concrete filled the hole to make a foundation strong enough to support both the pedestal and statue. At that time, it was the largest area of concrete ever poured in one place. Soon the pedestal began to rise on the foundation.

The pedestal fundraising committee asked the US Congress to pitch in the $100,000 more that was needed to finish it. They voted no. The committee tried other fundraising ideas. Bartholdi wrote and sold small booklets titled *The Statue of Liberty Enlightening the World*. Small copies of the Statue of Liberty were sold as souvenirs. A six-inch miniature cost one dollar, and a twelve-inch version was five dollars.

Many of the American committee members overseeing the construction of the pedestal were rich men. However, most weren't very generous when it came to giving their own money to the pedestal project. In October 1883, a newspaper publisher named Joseph Pulitzer became angry about this. In his national newspaper, *The World,* he complained that there were more than a hundred stingy millionaires in New York. They wouldn't miss the measly $100,000 needed to finish the pedestal. Why didn't they donate it? Maybe because they didn't want a statue that celebrated all people being equal.

By late 1883, the hand and torch had been shipped from America back to Paris to add to Bartholdi's statue. The head went on next. The statue was finished in January of 1884. Sadly, Edouard de Laboulaye had died in May of 1883. He never had the chance to see the finished statue.

The finished Liberty stood in Paris for one year waiting for its pedestal to be ready in New York. In August 1884, a newspaper artist drew a cartoon of the statue getting so tired of waiting that it had to sit down. In France, thousands of people came to visit the statue during this time, including a famous writer named Victor Hugo. French citizens were going to miss the statue!

Finally, in January of 1885, workers took the statue apart again. They unfastened every piece of copper and every piece of iron. The pieces were

packed into 214 crates, which each weighed from a few hundred pounds up to three tons. The crates were labeled with numbers so the statue could be put back together properly. If that ever happened. People were beginning to doubt that the pedestal would ever be finished. Without it, the statue had nothing to stand on.

In March 1885, building on the pedestal stopped on Bedloe's Island. The American committee had run out of money. Bartholdi was really worried. At the last minute his dream seemed to be falling apart.

Pulitzer was determined to fix the situation. He wrote articles in his newspaper that encouraged the everyday people of America to contribute to the pedestal fund. He wrote, "Let us not wait for the millionaires . . . Give something, however little." He promised to print the name of every contributor in his newspaper along with how much they gave.

To start things off, Pulitzer contributed $1,000 to the fund himself. In the first week, two thousand more dollars arrived at his offices. The donations usually came in coins totaling less than a dollar. Children gave the money they'd saved to go to the circus. Slowly, it all added up.

It was a thrill for people who donated to see their names printed in *The World*. They were famous for a day! It was good promotion for Pulitzer's newspaper, too. Hundreds of extra copies sold each day because anyone whose name was printed wanted a copy as a souvenir.

Encouraged by the donations, Bartholdi decided to send all the pieces of the statue to America. It took seventy train cars to haul the crates full of statue parts to the dock at Rouen, France. There, the crates were loaded onto a French ship named the *Isere* for the voyage to New York. This was a big job. Still, it was much easier than shipping a whole solid statue would have been. Statue ahoy!

Joseph Pulitzer

Born in Hungary on April 10, 1847, Joseph Pulitzer moved to the United States at age seventeen. His family was wealthy, but now he was alone and very poor. He taught himself to speak English. When someone cheated him out of five dollars, he wrote a story about it that was published in a small newspaper. Soon, he began working his way up. Pulitzer read at the library and studied law. He got his big break when he gave advice on a chess move to two newspaper editors during a game at the library. They helped him get a job as a reporter. By 1879, he'd bought two newspapers and combined them into the *St. Louis Post-Dispatch*.

Four years later he bought a bigger newspaper called *The New York World*. It had been losing money. Pulitzer turned it around by hiring the best reporters in America. One was a woman named

Nellie Bly. She became famous when she pretended to have a mental breakdown to get inside the Women's Lunatic Asylum and write stories of the terrible treatment of patients. Pulitzer's newspaper sales soared.

The Pulitzer Prizes are named after him. These awards are given out every year in categories of journalism, literature, music, and drama. It's a really big deal to win one.

CHAPTER 8
A Home in America

The *Isere* arrived in New York Harbor on June 17, 1885. It docked at Bedloe's Island two days later. Thousands of people in boats and onshore were waiting. They cheered and waved flags. It took several days to unload the crates, but there was no hurry because the pedestal wasn't ready!

It soon would be, thanks to the generosity of everyday Americans. In less than five months, about 121,000 Americans had donated a total of $102,000 to the pedestal fund. Pulitzer had done what he promised, printing every single name in the paper. On August 11, his newspaper's headline announced that the goal had been reached. Work on the pedestal started up again. It was finished by April of 1886.

Finally the 214 crates with pieces of the statue could be unpacked. Eiffel's iron structure was set up first and anchored deep in the pedestal. Then it was time to build the statue! It wouldn't be easy. Putting it together was like a puzzle. Some of the crates had been mislabeled back in France. Some of the pieces of copper and iron had become bent and needed reshaping.

Workers nicknamed the first rivet they pounded in place "Bartholdi" and the second one "Pulitzer." They climbed on Eiffel's iron tower like it was a huge jungle gym. They sat on the

crossbars and used ropes and pulleys to haul up pieces of copper. They sat on rope swings that dangled from the tower and pounded in over three hundred thousand rivets. From a distance,

you couldn't see the rivets or the seams where the copper sheets were joined. As the statue began to rise, the sole of the right foot was left open so they could use it as an entrance to the inside. New Yorkers and tourists often took small boats into the harbor to watch the work in progress.

Seven months after the pedestal was finished, the statue finally stood in place. It was the tallest man-made structure in the whole United States. In New York City, October 28, 1886, was declared a holiday to celebrate the statue. It was like a birthday party for Liberty! The day turned out to be rainy. Still, huge crowds came to watch a parade of twenty thousand people on Fifth Avenue that lasted all morning. Then hundreds of thousands of people jammed into lower Manhattan and stared toward the harbor, waiting for the statue to be unveiled.

French and American officials sailed to Bedloe's Island for the dedication ceremony. Almost all were men. The only women were the families of the French officials. Some people were angry about this and about the way women were treated in the US. After all, the Statue of Liberty *was* a woman! It symbolized freedom, but women in America still were not even free to vote. A group of women sailed a boat right up to Bedloe's Island to protest. They shouted at the politicians making speeches. However the celebration was so noisy that not many people heard them.

Everyone's attention was on the statue as ceremonies began on Bedloe's Island. A huge blue, white, and red striped French flag had been hung over the statue's face like a veil. For the grand finale, Bartholdi was supposed to pull the flag off. It wasn't easy to see the statue, especially from shore where crowds stood waiting. The sky was cloudy and misty. Steam from the boats in the harbor whooshed up and mixed with the drizzle.

FRANK LESLIE'S
ILLUSTRATED
NEWSPAPER

No. 1,551.—Vol. LX.] NEW YORK—FOR THE WEEK ENDING JUNE 13, 1885. [Price, 10 Cents.

1. OFFICIAL PRESENTATION OF THE STATUE OF "LIBERTY ENLIGHTENING THE WORLD," PARIS, JULY 6TH, 1884. 2. M. FRÉDÉRIC-AUGUSTE BARTHOLDI.
3. SECTIONAL VIEW OF STATUE, SHOWING IRON CORE AND BRACES.—SEE PAGE 271.
FRANCE-AMERICA.—THE GIFT OF THE FRENCH REPUBLIC TO THE UNITED STATES.

A newspaper covering the official presentation of the statue

Frédéric-Auguste Bartholdi

Bartholdi's original concept painting of the statue

TORCH PLATFORM ◆ +23'-9"

CROWN PLATFORM ◆ +267'-5"

LEVEL - 9S ◆ +232'-7 1/4"

LEVEL - 8S ◆ +221'-2 1/2"

LEVEL - 7S ◆ +211'-3/4"

LEVEL - 6S ◆ +207'-6"

LEVEL - 5S ◆ +199'-7 1/4"

LEVEL - 4S ◆ +176'-1"

MEZZANINE LEVEL - 1 ◆ +136'-5 1/4"

(A)

KEY

NOTE: REDRAWN, BASED ON 1984 ENGINEERING DRAWINGS
UNABLE TO VERIFY LOCATION OF INTERIOR
STRUCTURE TO EXTERIOR FEATURES
*EXCLUDING INTERIOR OF CROWN PLATFORM
(A) STRUCTURE UNCONFIRMED

STATUE - SECTION C-C

SCALE: FEET: 3/16"=1'-0"
METERS: 1:64

DELINEATED BY: ADAM EVERETT, 2006, RYAN PIERCE, DANA LOCKETT, 2011

| STATUE OF LIBERTY RECORDING PROJECT | ADDENDUM TO: STATUE OF LIBERTY, 1886 | SHEET | HISTORIC AMERICAN ENGINEERING RECORD |
| NATIONAL PARK SERVICE UNITED STATES DEPARTMENT OF THE INTERIOR | NEW YORK | LIBERTY ISLAND NEW YORK COUNTY | NEW YORK|32™36 | NY-138 |

A cross-section drawing from the back of the statue

TORCH
PLATFORM — ±278'-4"

CROWN
PLATFORM — ±267'-6"

LEVEL - 9S — ±232'-7 1/4"

LEVEL - 8S — ±221'-2 1/2"

LEVEL - 7S — ±211'-3/4"

LEVEL - 6S — ±200'-6"

LEVEL - 5S — ±188'-7 1/4"

LEVEL - 4S — ±178'-1"

MEZZANINE
LEVEL - 7P — ±13F-5 1/4"

KEY

NOTE: REDRAWN, BASED ON 1984 ENGINEERING DRAWINGS
UNABLE TO VERIFY LOCATION OF INTERIOR
STRUCTURE TO EXTERIOR FEATURES

STATUE - SECTION D-D   SCALE : FEET: 3/16=1'-0"
                                 METERS: 1:64

DELINEATED BY: CORY EDWARDS, 2006, RYAN PIERCE, DANA LOCKETT, 2011

STATUE OF LIBERTY RECORDING PROJECT		ADDENDUM TO: STATUE OF LIBERTY, 1886	SHEET	HISTORIC AMERICAN
NATIONAL PARK SERVICE		LIBERTY ISLAND		ENGINEERING RECORD
UNITED STATES DEPARTMENT OF THE INTERIOR	NEW YORK	NEW YORK COUNTY	NEW YORK 33 OF 36	NY-138

A cross-section drawing from the side of the statue

The face of the statue
removed from its crate

An elevator at the
bottom of the statue

Bartholdi and workers building the final
wood-and-plaster model of the statue's left hand

Gustave Eiffel's
supporting structure
for the statue

Pieces of the statue being prepared for assembly on Bedloe's Island in 1885

Workers constructing the statue in Bartholdi's Paris workshop

Spiral staircase at the
base of the statue

"LIBERTY ENLIGHTENING THE WORLD"
INAUGURATION OF THE BARTHOLDI STATUE. HARBOR OF NEW YORK

A photograph of the military and naval salute as President Grover
Cleveland arrives at Liberty Island for the statue's inauguration

An illustration of the dedication celebration in 1886

A newspaper illustration of crowds watching the arrival of the ships carrying the pieces of the statue

The head of the statue on display in a Paris park

British children sent to the United States during World War II wave to the statue as their ship enters New York Harbor

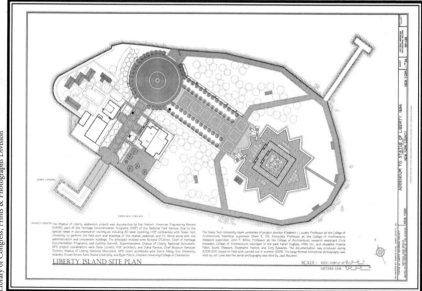

Liberty Island plan

An invitation to the inauguration of the statue

Visitors climbing to the observation
deck within the head of the statue

View of New York City from inside the crown

Scaffolding covering the statue during the 1984–1986 restoration

A 1984 photograph of the
statue's torch and hand

The Statue of Liberty

Bartholdi took the stairs up through the statue to stand outside on the balcony around its torch. He waited there for a signal. Far below him, politicians were making speeches about their love for the United States, and about friendship and freedom. President Grover Cleveland was supposed to speak soon.

There was some confusion about what happened next. Someone accidentally signaled Bartholdi at the wrong time. Before the president had a chance to give a speech, Bartholdi pulled the rope that was attached to the French flag. The flag fell away, revealing Lady Liberty's face to cheering crowds.

Women's Rights

In the late 1800s, women in the US still didn't have the same rights as men. Suffragists were people who demanded that women be allowed to vote. They also wanted women to be able to own property and be hired to do the same jobs as men. Susan B. Anthony, Elizabeth Cady Stanton, Sojourner Truth, and others made speeches in support of their cause. Amelia Bloomer wore loose pants called bloomers instead of the uncomfortable floor-length skirts of the 1800s. Wyoming was the first US territory to give women the right to vote in 1869. In 1920, the Nineteenth Amendment to the US Constitution was ratified, giving all female citizens the right to vote. As for France—where Liberty came from—women did not get to vote until 1945! There are still countries in the world today where women do not have same rights as men.

Navy ships fired guns as a salute. Steamship whistles blew. Bands began to play. The speeches continued in spite of the uproar. The celebration went on and on into the night.

It had taken twenty-one years to turn an interesting idea into an actual 151-foot statue. Bartholdi proudly told reporters, "The dream of my life is accomplished."

CHAPTER 9
The New Colossus

In 1883 Emma Lazarus wrote a fourteen-line poem, called a sonnet, that she named "The New Colossus." At the time, Jewish people in Russia were forced to flee their country or be killed, all because of their religion. Lazarus was upset about this and helped the Jewish immigrants arriving

in America. The troubles of these Russian Jews inspired her to write the poem. She donated it to an auction to raise money for the statue's pedestal.

After Lazarus died in 1887, a friend of hers accidentally found a copy of the poem printed in a book. She had the poem engraved on a plaque. The words told of people's struggles to reach America and find freedom. What better place to hang the plaque than at the Statue of Liberty!

Today Lazarus's poem is famous and the plaque is in the statue's museum. These are some of the lines from the poem engraved on the plaque:

"Give me your tired, your poor,
Your huddled masses yearning to breathe free,
The wretched refuse of your teeming shore.
Send these, the homeless, tempest-tost to me,
I lift my lamp beside the golden door!"

Lazarus called the Statue of Liberty the

"Mother of Exiles." In other words, it was like a mother who would take care of immigrants when they had no place else to go. The statue wasn't built with immigrants in mind. However, between 1892 and 1954, over twelve million immigrants reached America on ships that passed right by Bartholdi's statue. Standing on Bedloe's Island, it seemed to welcome newcomers to the United States, land of freedom and liberty. Early immigrants wrote home to their families about the statue. Some called it a welcoming goddess. The statue became a legend. Many immigrants and their families have written grateful letters to the Statue of Liberty itself!

Still, by the time Bartholdi died in 1904, most Americans didn't know what his statue looked like. It wasn't until World War I began in 1914 that the US government used Lady Liberty's picture on patriotic war posters. That's when Americans saw the posters everywhere. Soon the

Statue of Liberty was considered an important American symbol of freedom.

HELLO!
THIS IS LIBERTY SPEAKING
BILLIONS OF DOLLARS ARE NEEDED
AND NEEDED NOW

Bartholdi's statue became an official national monument in 1924. Bedloe's Island was given a new name in 1956: Liberty Island. This would have made Bartholdi happy, because he'd rooted for this new name.

The only way to reach Liberty Island today is by special ferryboats. Private boats are not allowed to dock there. You can also take a virtual tour of the statue at: http://www.nps.gov/stli/photosmultimedia/virtualtour.htm.

The wraparound observation deck at the top of the pedestal is as far as you can go without a special pass to the statue's crown. Only ten to fifteen people are allowed inside at a time. From the crown's windows, you can get an up-close look at the statue's right hand and torch. Plus there's a great view of New York City and the harbor. Visitors are no longer allowed to climb up to the torch.

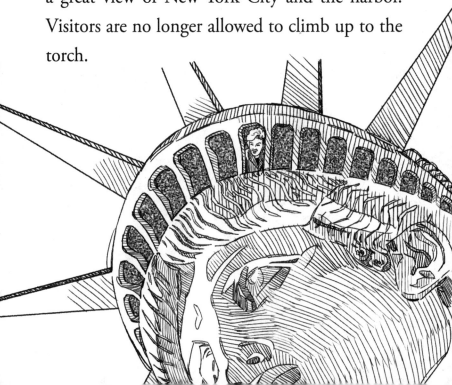

In 1976, the US celebrated its two-hundredth Independence Day. There were parades and fireworks in cities all over America. In New York, historic ships from thirty-two countries paraded past the Statue of Liberty. Millions of people watched on TV and from the streets of lower Manhattan. What many sadly noticed was that the ninety-year-old statue was in very bad shape.

CHAPTER 10
Spiffing Up the Statue

In 1980, two men illegally climbed the Statue of Liberty to hang a protest flag. After they came down, workers went up to check to see if they'd caused any damage. The rock climbing gear the protestors had used had not hurt anything much. However, it was discovered that the statue needed repair from top to bottom!

In the beginning, the statue had been the orange-brown color of a new copper penny. Copper doesn't rust or corrode. It protects itself by forming a blue-green coating called a patina on its surface. After ninety years, weather, salt air, and seawater had turned the copper statue permanently blue-green. That wasn't a problem, but the fact that it was streaked and stained from

bird poop and pollution *was* a problem. There were even bird nests in the folds of the statue's gown. Rust had gathered inside the statue on the iron bars that supported the copper panels. Some of the bars had completely crumbled away. Rivets had fallen out. The statue's eye was cracked and it had lost a piece of its hair. One of the pointed rays on the statue's crown was loose and had bent to poke the arm holding the torch.

There were big problems with the torch, too. Bartholdi had given it a copper skin flame. He hoped that would be covered in real gold someday.

However, Americans had been promised that the statue would be a lighthouse, so two rows of round holes were cut in the sculpted flame in 1886 and lights placed inside. The new lights turned out to be too dim to guide ships though.

Thirty years later, the torch was damaged when German soldiers sneaked into New York Harbor during World War I. They blew up tons of ammunition. A sculptor name Gutzon Borglum was hired to fix the torch. Later he would become famous for carving the heads of four presidents into Mount Rushmore.

Borglum cut about 250 angled windows in the copper flame and filled them with yellow-orange glass panes. This was not enough to make the statue an effective lighthouse, but everyone had given up on that idea back in 1902.

What no one realized was that Borglum's new design let water leak into the torch. Rainwater trickled down into the statue for years, causing its iron structure to rust. Where copper touched the iron, a chemical reaction had occurred, making more rust. Eiffel had shielded these metals from each other so that wouldn't happen, but time had worn away the shielding.

New York Harbor could get stormy with winds blowing fifty miles an hour. In strong winds, the statue swayed three inches side to side. The torch swayed as much as six inches. Eiffel had designed his structure to be flexible enough to allow for this movement. The thin iron bars that connected his pylon tower to the copper skin would bend slightly without breaking in strong wind or extreme temperatures. With the leaking torch, however, the iron structure was rusted and weak. The arm holding the torch would eventually have fallen off! Something had to be done fast.

Mount Rushmore

In 1924, a state historian named Doane Robinson asked Gutzon Borglum to carve a sculpture into the Black Hills of South Dakota. Robinson wanted one so amazing that it would attract lots of tourists. Borglum decided to carve four presidents on a sunlit granite wall of Mount Rushmore. He chose presidents that he thought best represented the first one-hundred-and-fifty years of US history—George Washington, Thomas Jefferson, Abraham Lincoln, and Theodore Roosevelt. After the US government agreed to fund the project, Borglum and his crew began sculpting it in 1927 using dynamite, hammers, drills, chisels, and other tools. When Borglum died just months before the carving was finished, his son completed it in 1941. The four heads are enormous. George Washington's head is as tall as a six-story building. His nose is taller than three men stacked on top of one another. Today, Mount Rushmore is South Dakota's top tourist attraction.

In 1981, experts were called in. They made a plan to repair almost every inch of the statue. A scaffold was built around it all the way up to the torch. The first workers who climbed up kissed the statue. They felt honored to be repairing this beloved landmark. The iron bars of the skeleton were replaced with stainless steel, which wouldn't rust. New heat and cooling systems were installed. A new and better spiral staircase was installed, too.

Over the years tourists had signed their names on the inside of the statue. The copper plates were cleaned and treated with a protective coating, but graffiti made by workers who built the statue in 1886 was not removed. At some point, someone had carved a message inside the statue's big toe that read: "Alone with God and the statue, Christmas Eve." There was even a "B" carved into a rivet by Bartholdi himself.

Along the way, workers discovered that when the statue was built, the head and right arm had been positioned about eighteen inches off center. This was not part of Eiffel's original plan and it weakened the structure. Still, it would be hard to change now. It was decided to keep the mistake to preserve history, but repairs were made and additional support was added.

However, the original torch was too far-gone to repair. It was taken down and is now in the lobby where visitors to the statue can see it up close. French metalworkers made an exact copy of the original copper skin torch using the repoussé method. The copper flame was then covered in twenty-four karat gold! By day, sunlight reflects

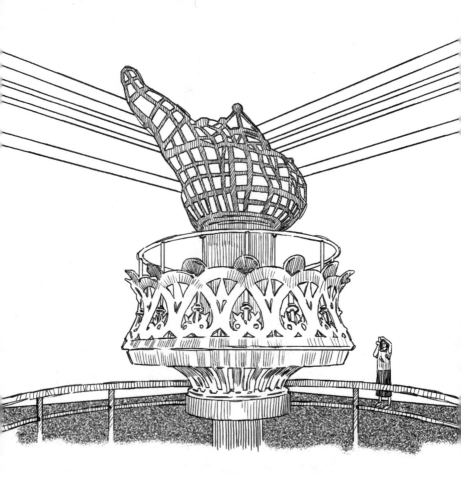

off the gold and by night the torch is lit with floodlights, making it appear to burn brightly. It's exactly what Bartholdi had wanted.

After two-and-a-half years, the repairs were finished in time for Fourth of July weekend, 1986.

The Statue of Liberty was one hundred years old! In New York there was a giant celebration called Liberty Weekend. Around thirty thousand small boats and ships filled New York Harbor. There was a huge street fair in New York. There were shows with gymnasts, marching bands, balloons, and famous singers.

Whitney Houston

The night of July 4, President Ronald Reagan stood with First Lady Nancy Reagan. He pressed a button to send colored laser beams that lit up the statue. More and more floodlights came on around Lady Liberty, slowly bathing her in light. Her torch was lit last of all. Brilliant red, white, and blue fireworks went off in a dramatic, dazzling finale. The future of the statue looked bright.

Just fifteen years later, something terrible happened. On September 11, 2001, two airplanes attacked the two buildings called the Twin Towers. These mammoth buildings stood in lower Manhattan across the harbor from the Statue of Liberty. The towers collapsed. Almost three thousand people died. It was the work of terrorists in a group called Al Qaeda. The US was their enemy. It was an awful time for the whole nation.

There was worry that the famous Statue of Liberty might be the next target of these terrorists. What if someone pretending to be a tourist came in and set off a bomb? So Liberty Island was closed temporarily.

Still, the Statue of Liberty held its torch high in New York Harbor and gave many sad Americans hope. During that horrible crisis, Lady Liberty still stood and was reopened to visitors in 2009.

The French had created the statue to honor the strong, democratic government of the United States. Like the American flag, the statue became a symbol of the nation. Its message encourages freedom for everyone throughout the world. It stands tall and proud. It stands for liberty!

How Big Is the Statue of Liberty?

Location	Measurement
Statue, pedestal, and foundation combined height	305'1"
Statue's base to torch's tip	151'1"
Head height	17'3"
Eye width	2'6"
Nose length	4'6"
Mouth width	3'0"
Right arm length	42'0"
Hand length	16'5"
Index finger length	8'0"
Tablet length	23'7"
Tablet thickness	2'0"
Pedestal height	89'0"
Weight of copper skin	31 tons

Timeline of the Statue of Liberty

1865	Laboulaye and Bartholdi discuss giving a statue to the United States
1871	Bartholdi goes to America the promote the statue idea
1875	Bartholdi begins building the statue in Paris, France
	The hand and torch are exhibited at the Centennial Exposition in Philadelphia
1877	Bedloe's Island is officially chosen as the statue's site
1880	Gustave Eiffel designs the inner framework of the statue
1881	The copper plates and support framework are finished
1882	Laboulaye dies
	Lazarus writes "The New Colossus"
	The Statue of Liberty is completed in Paris
	Construction begins on the pedestal in the United States
	The statue is shipped to New York
	Pulitzer raises over $100,000 to finish the pedestal
	The statue is rebuilt on Bedloe's Island
	The statue is officially dedicated on October 28
1892	Ellis Island opens
1956	Bedloe's Island is renamed Liberty Island
1984	Two years of repairs begin on the statue
1986	Americans celebrate the Statue of Liberty's 100th anniversary
2019	The new Statue of Liberty Museum opens on Liberty Island

Timeline of the World

US Civil War ends	1865
President Lincoln is assassinated	
Alice's Adventures in Wonderland by Lewis Carroll is published	
Chemist Marie Curie is born	1867
Dynamite is invented by Alfred Nobel	
The Suez Canal opens	1869
P. T. Barnum's circus opens in Brooklyn	1871
Yellowstone becomes the first US National Park	1872
Mount Vesuvius volcano erupts in Italy	
Magician Harry Houdini is born in Hungary	1874
Alexander Graham Bell invents the telephone	1876
Mark Twain publishes *The Adventures of Tom Sawyer*	
Wild Bill Hickok is killed in Deadwood, South Dakota	
Albert Einstein is born	1879
Helen Keller is born	1880
Pablo Picasso is born	1881
The Brooklyn Bridge is completed	1883
Louis Pasteur makes a rabies vaccine	1885
Annie Oakley joins Buffalo Bill's Wild West show	
Basketball is invented	1891
The New York Stock Exchange crashes, sending the country into the Great Depression	1929
The United States celebrates its bicentennial on July 4	1976

Bibliography

*Books for young readers

Burns, Ken. *The Statue of Liberty*. DVD. PBS, 1985.

*Curlee, Lynn. *Liberty*. New York: Atheneum Books for Young Readers, 2000.

*Drummond, Allan. *Liberty!* New York: Frances Foster Books, 2002.

*Hochain, Serge. *Building Liberty: A Statue Is Born*. Washington, DC: National Geographic, 2004.

Khan, Yasmin Sabina. *Enlightening the World: The Creation of the Statue of Liberty*. Ithaca, NY: Cornell University Press, 2010.

Moreno, Barry. *The Statue of Liberty*. Images of America. Charleston, SC: Arcadia Publishing, 2004.

*Rappaport, Doreen. *Lady Liberty: A Biography*. Cambridge, MA: Candlewick Press, 2008.

Shapiro, Mary J. *Gateway to Liberty: The Story of the Statue of Liberty and Ellis Island*. New York: Vintage, 1986.

Skomal, Lenore. *Lady Liberty: The Untold Story of the Statue of Liberty*. Kennebunkport, ME: Cider Mill Press, 2009.

Sutherland, Cara A. *The Statue of Liberty*. New York: Barnes & Noble Books, 2003.

You can visit the official website of the Statue of Liberty at http://www.nps.gov/stli.

YOUR HEADQUARTERS FOR HISTORY

Activities, Mad Libs, and sidesplitting jokes!
Discover the Who HQ books beyond the biographies

Who? What? Where?

Learn more at whohq.com!